SNUG
AS A
BUG
Where Bugs Live

Inside the Worm's Hole

by Meish Goldish

Consultants:

Samuel James, PhD
Department of Biology, The University of Iowa

Kimberly Brenneman, PhD
National Institute for Early Education Research, Rutgers University, New Br

D1212985

BEARPORT
PUBLISHING

New York, New York

Credits

Cover, © Dwight Kuhn Photography; 2–3, © Pan Xunbin/Shutterstock; 4, © Nigel Cattlin/FLPA; 5, © Cappi Thompson/Shutterstock; 6–7, © antpkr/Shutterstock; 8, © Power and Syred/Science Photo Library; 9, © Animals Animals/Superstock; 10, © Nordic Photos/Superstock; 11, 12, © Dwight Kuhn Photography; 13, © Derek Middleton/FLPA; 14, © Bob Gibbons/FLPA; 15, © Dwight Kuhn Photography; 16, © Dickie Duckett/FLPA; 17, © Koo/Shutterstock; 18, © Pakhnyushcha/Shutterstock; 19, © Dwight Kuhn Photography; 20–21, © Gary K. Smith/FLPA; 21B, 22, 23TL, 23TC, © Dwight Kuhn Photography; 23TR, © Pakhnyushcha/Shutterstock; 23BL, © Davydova Svetlana/Shutterstock; 23BC, © ifong/Shutterstock; 23BR, © Power and Syred/Science Photo Library.

Publisher: Kenn Goin
Senior Editor: Joyce Tavolacci
Creative Director: Spencer Brinker
Design: Emma Randall
Photo Researcher: Ruby Tuesday Books

Library of Congress Cataloging-in-Publication Data

Goldish, Meish.
  Inside the worm's hole / by Meish Goldish.
     pages cm. — (Snug as a bug: where bugs live)
  Includes index.
  ISBN-13: 978-1-61772-904-1 (library binding)
  ISBN-10: 1-61772-904-3 (library binding)
  1. Earthworms—Juvenile literature. 2. Worms—Juvenile literature. I. Title.
  QL391.A6G65 2014
  592'.64—dc23
                          2013005029

For more information, write to Bearport Publishing Company, Inc., 45 West 21st Street, Suite 3B, New York, New York 10010. Printed in the United States of America.

10 9 8 7 6 5 4 3 2 1

Contents

What's in That Hole?

It's a cool summer night in a vegetable garden.

Suddenly, an earthworm wriggles out of the dirt through a tiny hole in the ground.

With its tail end still in the soil, the worm searches for food nearby.

Before sunrise, the wiggly creature will return to its underground home.

Why do you think a worm returns to its hole before the sun appears?

earthworm

worm's hole

earthworm

Earthworms have soft bodies and no arms or legs.

Moist Homes

Earthworms spend most of their lives in cool, damp soil.

They stay underground during the day to keep away from the hot sun.

If their skin dries out, they will die.

At night, however, it's cool enough for the worms to leave their hidden homes.

Arctic Ocean

North America

Atlantic Ocean

Pacific Ocean

South America

Europe

Africa

Asia

Indian Ocean

Australia

Southern Ocean

Antarctica

N
W   E
S

Where earthworms live

wet skin

Earthworms range in length from only one inch (2.5 cm) to more than eight feet (2.4 m).

Moving Forward

As a worm moves through the ground, it makes tunnels.

Although the worm's body is soft, it can still push itself through the soil.

The worm crawls by first stretching out the front part of its body.

Then it pulls its tail end forward.

Tiny hairs on the worm's skin, called **setae**, grab the dirt to help the worm move forward.

setae

close-up of a worm

Some earthworms live close to the top of the ground. Others, such as nightcrawlers, dig tunnels more than six feet (1.8 m) deep.

tunnel

Breaking Up Soil

As a worm crawls underground, its long body breaks up the soil.

Its body also makes tiny holes in the dirt.

Air and rainwater travel through these holes to reach the **roots** of plants.

The roots take in the air and water that plants need to grow.

young plant

plant roots

If an earthworm finds a small rock blocking its path underground, it pushes it aside. A worm can move a rock that's up to 50 times its own weight!

Eating Along the Way

A worm finds food as it moves through the dirt.

It eats soil and tiny pieces of dead plants.

The food the earthworm eats passes through its body.

Then the food comes out of the worm's tail end as droppings, or **castings**.

worm eating pumpkin

A worm eats leaves, seeds, fruits, vegetables, and roots.

worm castings

How do you think the worm's castings help plants grow?

Worm Droppings

A worm's castings are filled with **nutrients**.

The nutrients come from the different plant parts that the worm ate.

Castings make soil rich and healthy.

They help the plants that live around a worm's hole grow bigger and taller.

grass growing in worm castings

After eating at night, a worm uses its castings to cover the entrance to its home. The castings hide the worm's hole.

castings at the entrance to a worm's hole

Why do you think a worm hides the entrance to its hole?

Danger Above and Below

Many different animals, such as toads, snakes, and skunks, feed on worms.

A hungry bird will try to tug a worm out of its hole to eat it.

However, pulling the slender creature out of the ground isn't so easy.

A worm uses its setae to hold itself firmly in place.

bird tugging on a worm

mole

worm

Animals that
live underground,
such as moles,
also hunt worms
for food.

17

Laying Eggs

In the spring, earthworms find **mates** so they can have babies.

After mating, each worm forms a **cocoon** around its body.

Up to six eggs slip out of the worm's body and into the cocoon.

Later, the entire cocoon falls off the worm's body.

Unlike most other animals, every worm is both male and female. After two earthworms mate, each one lays eggs and has babies.

worm cocoons

Room to Grow

After about three weeks, the eggs inside a cocoon hatch.

Each baby is less than one inch (2.5 cm) long and looks like a piece of thread.

Although tiny, the babies can dig their own holes without their parents' help.

It can take up to a year before worms are fully grown.

All the while, they'll be wiggling their way through the soil!

adult
earthworm

Some types
of worms can
live up to
20 years!

baby worm
hatching

cocoon

Science Lab

Be a Worm Scientist

Imagine you are a scientist who studies earthworms. Write a report about the worm's activities above and below the ground.

Begin the report by describing what the worm does during the day and then describe what the worm does at night. Use the information in this book to help you. Draw pictures to include in your report.

When you are finished, present your report and drawings to friends and family.

Here are some words you can use when writing about a worm's home and activities.

roots hole plants soil day

tunnels night leaves castings

Read the questions below and think about the answers. You can include the information from your answers in your report.

- *How does a worm make tunnels?*

- *Why does a worm stay in the ground during the day? What does a worm do above the ground at night?*

- *How do worms help plants grow?*

Science Words

castings (KAST-ingz)
waste that passes out of a
worm's body after it eats

cocoon (kuh-KOON)
a hard shell on a worm's
body where eggs grow

mates (MAYTS) animals
that have young together

nutrients (NOO-tree-uhnts)
substances needed by plants
to grow and stay healthy

roots (ROOTS) the parts of
a plant that take in food
and water from the soil

setae (SET-ay) hairlike
parts on the outside of
a worm's body

Index

Read More

Llewellyn, Claire. *Earthworms.* New York: Franklin Watts (2002).

Lunis, Natalie. *Wiggly Earthworms (No Backbone! The World of Invertebrates).* New York: Bearport (2009).

Pfeffer, Wendy. *Wiggling Worms at Work.* New York: HarperCollins (2004).

Learn More Online

To learn more about worms and their holes, visit
www.bearportpublishing.com/SnugasaBug

About the Author

Meish Goldish has written more than 200 books for children. His book *Dolphins in the Navy* received a Eureka! Honor Book Award from the California Reading Association in 2012.